Aberdeen

Photographs by
Werner Hahn

Aberdeen
catching the last rays

Photographs by *Werner* Hahn
Text by Dean Barrett

The Perennial Press, Hong Kong

First Edition, 1974
Photographs Copyright © 1974 by Werner Hahn
Text Copyright © 1974 by Dean Barrett

Layout by Werner Hahn

Published by R.V. Pandit for
The Perennial Press, 704 Lee Hing Building,
Pottinger Street, Central, Hong Kong
Printed by Dai Nippon Printing Co. (Hong Kong) Ltd.
Library of Congress Catalogue Number 73-94260

the setting
past, present, future

the portrait
from *dawn* to dusk

the people
7 interviews

preface

When I first saw Aberdeen I shared the excitement that all photographers must feel on viewing the harbor and its people for the first time. I was drawn to it again and again until at last I decided to search out and photograph the moods and rhythms of its life. The assignment was a demanding one, and consumed over three years. Aberdeen changes from season to season, from day to day, nor does it readily reveal to the outsider its many faces. Each of Aberdeen's misty dawns is unique; each late afternoon's light fades in its own way; each workday forms its own fleeting patterns, shapes and colors, all in constant motion.

I find it astonishing that this floating community survives in a city like Hong Kong, where industrialization and modern architectural design are irrevocably eroding the colony's past. Yet, in most ways, Aberdeen stubbornly perpetuates its own past. One can still see the archetypical junks, sampans and hawker boats, filled with fruits, flowers and vegetables, that have floated there for generations. There are still the floating barbers, doctors, tailors and restaurants. Of course, Aberdeen is slowly changing. But the past's traditions are still carefully maintained by the people. The shrine of Tin Hau, Queen of Heaven and patron saint of the fisherfolk, can be found on every boat, and offerings and incense are still placed before the images of "Thousand Mile Eyes" and "Fair Wind Ears."

While exploring Aberdeen, I developed great respect for the sea gipsies and their society, whose rules are based on a fierce love of independence and a remarkable sense of tolerance. Unlike land people, who change residence, Aberdeen's boat dwellers live in one place and within the same circle of friends. Their boats are their permanent homes, the harbor is their permanent neighborhood. They have the strongest sense of community I have ever observed.

But, it is slowly yielding, just as, throughout Asia, many societies, once culturally strong, have disappeared beneath the customs and the trappings of the West. In Aberdeen, more and more fishing families are moving to land, trading their poop deck cubicles for the relative comfort of resettlement estates. The life of Aberdeen can now be measured not in generations but in years.

Aberdeen is a community bonded by strong beliefs and a commonalty of spirit. But it is doomed to vanish, like other cultures before it. Today, a magnificent big junk under full sail is rarely seen in the waters of Hong Kong. It is my hope that this book may acquaint others with the sea gipsies of South China before the last sun sets on Aberdeen.

Werner Hahn, April 1974

to my parents

the setting
past, present, future

In the last hours of darkness, even before the nets of the fishing junks glitter in the first rays of the morning sun, Aberdeen is awake, as she has been for centuries. Long before the colored lightbulbs and neon networks of floating restaurants illuminated her dirty pea-green water, before the patched sails of her fishing junks were outmoded by fuming diesel engines, before men dreamed of linking Apleichau, or Goose Tongue Island, to the mainland with a bridge soaring 50 feet above the ships' masts, before resettlement estates lined her hillsides, thinning her forests of masts and luring her people ashore forever. Even before the first British sailors replenished their supply of fresh water from the springs of nearby hillsides, Aberdeen was awake.

   Known to the Chinese for centuries as Heung Kong T'sai, or Little Hong Kong, Aberdeen's very survival offers testimony to the endurance of her people. The wrath of the gods has often plagued her in many forms: the "great winds" of relentless typhoons, sudden attacks of desperate pirates, raised nets inexplicably empty of their catch and, finally, the coming of the western "barbarian."

   For generations, the ocean's ceaseless swell has been her fishermen's cradle, and sometimes its dark depths became their tomb. Neither on its surface nor within its depths are there hidden diaries or tall monuments or ancient ruins to testify to their skills and courage over the centuries. No preserved footprints, or secluded paths, or long-forgotten trade routes will ever shed new light on their bold adventures. And their only conqueror — the sea — will never yield what it knows of their past hopes and fears, their conquests and their tragedies.

   The first fishermen in the Aberdeen area were probably descendants of the followers of the young Sung emperor who fled to Hong Kong in the late 13th century in an unsuccessful attempt to escape the armies of the Mongols. As the emperor fled south, some of his followers settled along the coastal regions of Kwangtung province. But many reached Hong Kong waters and, after their emperor's defeat, took up farming. They began to use the free months between harvests to fish in the coastal waters. This proved so profitable that farming was eventually abandoned. Thus the floating population of fishermen came into being.

   They believe that the head family of the early fishermen was descended from the Sung dynasty royal house of T'ang, or *T'ang Ke.* Through the centuries, animosity arose between the boat people and those who remained ashore. As a term of derision, the people on land corrupted the Chinese character for T'ang and began to use the disrespectful term of *t'an,* meaning egg. An egg is something which is not quite developed, so their meaning was clear. The name *Tanka*

With the cession of Hong Kong to the British in 1841, Aberdeen's aspect began its transformation, slowly at first, and then more and more rapidly. At the turn of the century, junks with full sails, far left, were still a common sight. The fishermen of Aberdeen have always been at the mercy of the weather, as illustrated in the picture at left, showing the Aberdeen docks after a typhoon. In the picture below, the seashore of Apleichau Island bustles around the Hung Shing Temple, built by local fisherfolk in 1773. The two 60-foot spirit poles before the temple can still be seen today.

has persisted to this day, but much of the animosity originally connected with the term has faded. The boat people call themselves *shui-jen,* or "water folk." The sampan dwellers are mostly Hakkas; the junk fishermen are Hoklos from various counties of China's Kwangtung province and from Hong Kong itself. Some, however, are from as far west as Hainan and others have traveled from as far east as Fukien.

For centuries their fishing junks plied the waters of Southeast China's irregular coastline; Aberdeen's harbor served as shelter and home port. Whether they felt the more primitive boat people might compete for their land or whether acting simply in envy of their freedom, the mainland Chinese devised laws forbidding the seafarers to reside on land. Nor could they intermarry with those who lived ashore. Along with merchants, actors and criminals, they were also denied the opportunity of competing in China's Examination System, thereby losing any hope of attaining the status of officials.

The land people scorned them with tales of sea gipsies possessing six toes on each foot, with green eyes that could see dragons and other ferocious creatures lurking in the sea's murky depths; gipsies who could swim for miles without tiring or dive deep into the ocean.

In the reign of the Ch'ing dynasty emperor K'ang Hsi (AD 1662-1722), notice was given that the boat people might henceforth erect dwellings on river banks. But by then the fishermen had come to regard those on land as followers of a less exalted way of life, and they wanted no part of it. Besides, if they could not partake in the pleasures of mainland life, neither did they share in its pains; their need to jump from boat to boat assured the women of the fishing settlements that their feet would remain unbound.

Aberdeen is one of the island's oldest settlements. Its name — Hong Kong T'sai — may be translated as "Little Fragrant Harbor" or "Incense Bay."

Some of Aberdeen's more elderly residents say that the "fragrance" referred to the sweet-smelling sandalwood used in the building of ships; others, equally venerable, point to the great supply of incense shipped to Canton as the true origin of the name. One tale traces it to the fresh — hence, "fragrant" — spring water found just to the west of present-day Aberdeen in the nearby cove of Shekpaiwan, or Stone-lined Bay. No one knows for sure.

When ocean-going ships arrived from the west, the mariners refilled their water-casks at a stream in the hills. The sailors heard the name "Hong Kong" and mistakenly believed that it applied to the whole island. Soon it appeared on their charts and in the treaties following the opium wars of the early 1840s. Still later, the

As in the Chinnery School sketch at right, Chinese boat girls have proved popular subjects for artists. The drawing at upper right was executed in 1846. Its subject is the south side of Aberdeen Harbor looking east. The 1838 drawing of the harbor scene at extreme right depicts the dwellings of the poor.

12

name was applied to the entire British colony, including Kowloon and the New Territories.

An account of Aberdeen was written during a visit of Lord Amherst's fleet which took the British Ambassador to Peking in 1816. The ships anchored at Shekpaiwan, or Aberdeen Harbor, which the writer described as affording "admirable shelter for ships of any burden." The inhabitants he saw were "some poor weather-beaten fishermen spreading their nets, and drying the produce of their toils, on the rocks which supported their miserable huts."

A watercolor of the "Waterfall at Hong Cong" was made from the deck of H.M.S. Alceste. British sailors knew the site as Waterfall Bay, a name now used to describe another location. And what little remains of the waterfall itself now carries the overflow from the Aberdeen reservoir to a point east of the town.

It was then fashionable to name places of new colonies after prominent statesmen. And so the British Foreign Secretary, Lord Aberdeen, was chosen for the honor. The Secretary had been in office during the cession of the colony in 1841. It is an ironic quirk of history that Lord Aberdeen opposed the acquisition.

Soon after the British arrival, Aberdeen was developed into an important center for shipbuilding; by 1857 it boasted a dry dock. In 1879 another traveler was able to refer to Aberdeen as "a town which has grown up around the Hong Kong docks, where we saw a huge American steamer undergoing repairs." But fame and importance did not linger long on the fishing settlement. The British settlers soon moved on, up into the hills, and, in the course of time, completely around the island. Aberdeen was soon eclipsed by the island's Victoria district, which the British chose as their center of activity. Across from their settlement, on the shore of the Kowloon peninsula, pirates, posing as fishermen, waited to attack all vessels entering the narrow Lye Mun Pass. But with the advent of British sea power, the pirates' days were numbered.

The population of the boat people has risen and fallen with the tides of East Asian history. An 1856 census tells us that 2,343 persons worked aboard 415 boats. Ten years later, 4,130 persons worked aboard 424 boats. With the passing of the years, the waters around Hong Kong became ever more popular as a fishing ground. Fishermen based in Macao or China regarded Aberdeen as both a marketing place and safe anchorage.

After the Japanese invasion of China and the subsequent fall of Canton, Hong Kong's floating population grew; houseboats, junks, sampans and barges crowded the bay. In the face of hostile armadas, Aberdeen's fishermen found deep sea fishing too dangerous, but the colony's waters continued to yield abundant catches.

Then, without warning, in December 1941, Japanese bombs rained destruction upon Hong Kong. For nearly four years, Japanese will was law; it was the boat people who suffered the most. They were forced to load and unload vessels and to bow in the presence of their conquerors. Worst of all, the harbor was closed. But despite bombings and highly effective machine gun fire, some vessels managed to sneak to Macao and to China under cover of darkness. The waterfolk soon became experts at making false bottoms to loot cargo. Goods destined for unfriendly hands were often thrown overboard. But the once-bustling harbor became a graveyard of ships and the fishing industry collapsed. Hundreds of junks were lost, fishing as an occupation was all but abandoned and the fishermen were mired in debt.

It was then that the Hong Kong government first began to coordinate the industry, arranging for loans and setting up a marketing organization which greatly benefited the fishermen. The Fish Marketing Organization, a non-government trading group controlled by the Director of the Agriculture and Fisheries Department, was one of several postwar innovations designed to help rebuild the fleet. The Organization took control of several wholesale fish markets on Hong Kong Island, in Kowloon and in the New Territories, offered fishermen financial assistance to improve their vessels and equipment, established schools for their children and aided in transporting the fish to the wholesale markets. Classes organized by the Fisheries Division were adapted to the schedule of the fishermen. Soon, men whose entire learning had been passed from generation to generation almost without change were studying marine engineering, boat design, navigation and recent inventions in fishing equipment.

All has not gone smoothly, of course. When the first schools were opened for the children of fishermen, the children were afraid to mix with the land people; separate classes were held for them. Even today, many fishermen prefer the old methods of fishing to anything new.

From 1911 until 1948, the colony's boat population steadily increased. With the founding of the People's Republic of China in 1949, a new allegiance was demanded of the fishermen who cruised their traditional fishing grounds in China's waters. The proportion of a catch demanded by their mother country was so great that many junks forfeited their Chinese licenses and, avoiding Chinese shore patrol vessels, departed to Hong Kong. Between 1957 and 1962, the colony's fishing fleet swelled from 6,000 vessels to more than 10,000. In recent years, China's demands have moderated, and assistance as well as ready markets are again available in her ports and fishing villages.

Aberdeen has approximately 2,000 boats in its harbor with another 2,000 vessels constantly passing through, whose families regard Aberdeen as "home port." In all, some 25,000 people live aboard. It is this constant appearance and disappearance of vessels which accounts for the great disparity in estimates of Aberdeen's floating population.

Whatever their number, those who make their living from the sea retain their traditions; and, even today, the fisherman's most colorful traditions are preserved in his festivals.

To the water folk, festivals are still celebrated with great enthusiasm and with scrupulous attention to detail. Hong Kong's floating cities are scenes of great excitement during such occasions as the Dragon Boat Festival with its lively boat races; the festival in honor of Tam Kung, the god who controls the winds; the birthday of Hung Shing, the deity who predicts the weather, and the Festival of the Hungry Ghosts, designed to appease the spirits of all the dead who have no known graves. Many boat people lost their lives during Japanese bombings and special attention is paid to this last festival.

The most important of their festive occasions is held in honor of Tin Hau, Queen of Heaven, and patroness of seafarers. At first light, on the 23rd night of the third moon, junk pilgrimages are made to the Great Temple in Joss House Bay and to other temples on Hong Kong's shores, where the goddess sits gazing out upon

the water in constant watch over her people. Ironically — and, as many of Aberdeen's fishermen believe, ominously — Aberdeen's own Tin Hau temple, built by local fishing families in 1851, no longer stands on the shore; reclamation has pushed it inland.

In temples dedicated to Tin Hau, she is often accompanied by her attendants "Thousand Mile Eyes" and "Fair Wind Ears." On the day of the festival, small flotillas of vessels gaily decorated with brightly colored flags, streamers and floral screens visit the temples. Celebrations in her honor include performances of Chinese opera, lion dances, fireworks, smoldering joss sticks offerings of sacrificial roast pigs covered with banners and flowers, models of ships, chickens, dishes of pink buns and baskets of red eggs, and money. While smoke from hundreds of burning joss sticks keeps eyes watering, the deafening sounds of cymbals and drums assail the ears.

The shrines to Tin Hau are carefully carried onto the land and into the temples. Offerings are made. Later, they are returned to their places of honor aboard the junks. The vessels also carry large wood and paper decorations known as *fa pau* specially made for the occasion. The beautiful figures of the *fa pau* are considered to be lucky possessions and they are later auctioned. The frame of the *fa pau* itself is burned.

Naturally, the festivals soon give way to the serious business of making a living. The junks are cleared of decoration and each person again assumes the function assigned to him for the voyage. Where the junk sails and for how long depends on its class. As the fishermen know from lifetimes of experience, "junk" is merely a generic term for innumerable types of Chinese sailing vessels. The name probably had its origin in the Fukinese word *ch'un* (Cantonese *shuen*). The Indonesians modified it to *djong;* and, to the Dutch, it became *jonk.* With various modifications, the term spread throughout Europe and elsewhere. In his memoirs, Marco Polo describes the junks of China's Yuan dynasty (AD 1279-1368) which were already sailing to Sumatra, India and the Persian Gulf.

Depending on the season, Aberdeen's junks may go out after 20 kinds of fish, including shark. The fishing season extends from October to May, the other four months comprising the typhoon season. But now that the junks are motorized, the larger ones can go out for one or two weeks even during the typhoon season. They travel as far west as Hainan, east to Quemoy and even to Vietnam.

With its shape under almost constant modification, the most meaningful classification of the junk is by its function. Trawling is probably the colony's most popular method of fishing. The deep-sea trawlers generally work in pairs and carry crews of ten or more. They drag a huge

Chinese junks in the harbor (upper left).
The old Tin Hau Temple in Causeway Bay, far left, is one of many temples dedicated to the Heavenly Queen. This patroness of seafarers is the chief protective deity of the boat people. The photograph of the beggar outside the temple was taken in 1870, before reclamation pushed the temple well away from the harbor.
Overleaf: Long before modernization provided the sea gipsies with diesel engines, hundreds of junks with full sails transformed the harbor of Aberdeen into a traditional Chinese scene of romantic beauty.

bag-shaped net along the seabed, gathering in red sea bream, lizard fish and sole, horse-head and red snapper, red goatfish and golden thread. The fish swim along the sea bottom and seldom escape the conical bag of netting, which may extend to 250 feet.

Purse-seiners also work in pairs but remain fairly close to shore. By their attraction to the fishermen's bright lights, small fish such as carangoid, anchovies, green pilchard, golden sardine and pomfret are lured near the surface into a trapezoidal-shaped net stretched vertically between the junks. Sometimes dozens of junks work together using drag seines up to 4,000 feet long. The fishermen may also thrash the water with long-handled pummels. If fish are scarce, they may even resort to illegally stunning the fish by explosives.

In gill netting, long rectangular gill nets are laid across the currents for white herring, yellow croaker, mackerel, jewfish, tongue soles and hair-tails. The gills of the fish are entangled in the mesh of the net. Gill-netters also hang their nets vertically between two junks or between one junk and a buoy or a fixed point on shore. Their catches consist of mackerel, flatfish, white herring and yellow croaker.

Liners are either simple hook-fishing affairs or else long-liners which lay lengths of line, bearing hundreds of hooks, along the sea bottom.

About 24 hours after the lines are set, they are pulled up. Their catch consists of conger pike, white herring, lizard fish, cuttlefish, flatfish, garoupa and golden thread.

In addition to the common methods of trawling, seining, gill-netting and lining, there are other, more exotic, methods, some of which are fast disappearing. These include the use of decoy fish made of sandalwood dragged through the water; wooden clappers and flares to frighten fish into a net and, finally, the use of offshore and inshore nets. A few miles from Lantao there is a rock where, it is said, the God-spirit of the *Wong Fa,* or yellow flower fish, dwells. During November and December, great shoals of these fish converge in the area of the rock. Fishermen with experienced ears listen at the side of their junks or through the bottom boards of a sampan. Once the fish are located, great numbers are netted.

Besides Aberdeen, Hong Kong Island's other centers of floating communities are at Shaukeiwan and Causeway Bay. Kowloon has Yaumati Typhoon Shelter and the New Territories has Sai Kung. A large community is also found at Cheung Chau Island and at Tai Po on Lantao.

Aberdeen itself is well protected by surrounding hills. Clusters of boats crowd the harbor and board-walks run between one cluster and the next. In the safety of the harbor, sails are mended, nets are dried, and the events of the last fishing

On the fifth day of the fifth lunar month, the Dragon Boats race. The centuries-old tradition began as an attempt to cause the heavenly dragons to fight, bringing rains for the crops. The pictures at right were taken in Aberdeen Harbor about a century ago. Since then, both the hair styles of the racers and the scenery of Aberdeen have undergone great changes. Like Aberdeen, Hong Kong's other fishing villages have been renowned for their picturesque beauty. At upper right, Shaukeiwan Bay and the Taikoo dock are seen as they appeared c. 1920. At lower right is Yaumati, another settlement of Hong Kong's boat people. In the photograph, taken c. 1880, Lion Rock looms in the background.

trip are discussed. Small sampans weave constantly to and fro, narrowly avoiding dozens of collisions a day. To the *east*, the pleasure craft of affluent men of the land bob up and down, reflecting the sunlight.

Just across the harbor, behind the colorful floating restaurants, are the low green hills of Apleichau Island. The small, narrow main street serves as passageway, marketplace and playground. Dozens of boat-building yards and small metal-work shops line its shores. A huge electric power station dominates the southern part of the island.

Near the island's tiny pier, the Hung Shing temple is only a five-minute ferry ride from Aberdeen's shore. Its patrons are almost exclusively local fisherfolk, whose ancestors built the temple during the Ch'ing dynasty in 1773, the 38th year of the reign of Ch'ien Lung. On March 17, 1973 a great celebration marked the 200th anniversary of the monument, which honors a legendary official who lived more than a thousand years ago. He is said to have learned the secrets of predicting the weather, which greatly aided the fishermen. The fishermen believe that he died of overwork, but that his spirit continues to guard many from typhoons and other disasters. The two 60-foot poles before the temple protect the local fishing families from evil spirits or tigers, which the surrounding hills are said to represent. The island also has a small century-old temple dedicated to *Kuan Yin*, the Goddess of Mercy.

Every year, Aberdeen's 100 boatyards build nearly 300 fishing boats, including sailing junks. Many of the boats being built for the fishermen are not designed for them to live on. The waterfolk will continue to go to sea but will live on the land. While it is true the Hong Kong government discourages people from living on their boats, the more successful fishermen themselves prefer to send their families to live on shore.

More than a dozen different types of junks are made here and, with their high poop deck, counter-stern and large, perforated rudder, none of them bears more than a superficial resemblance to any of those built in China. The junks range in size from a one-masted 35-footer to a 95-footer complete with midship's mainmast, foremast and small aftermast on the poop. A small junk may take only a month to build, a large one up to six months. The junk's high, flat stern and low bow give the impression of an extraordinarily low hull burrowing its way through the water. It is this high stern and lack of proper ballast which makes it unsuitable on the high seas. However, as a lighter for loading cargo within the safety of a harbor, it is well-designed.

While the boatyards are always active, the hub of all Aberdeen's activities is the Aberdeen Wholesale Fish Market which comes to life every morning at 5. Fish of every color and length imaginable — and some unimaginable — are auctioned: the beautiful golden thread, the fierce conger pike with dagger teeth, the red sea bream with a red swelling between the eyes, the lizard fish with its strange mouth lined with teeth, anchovies, all varieties of sea snakes, sharks and manta rays, and the yellow croaker.

As each fish is offered, the stage is set for lively bidding: crabs, mackerel, sole, crayfish, herring, shrimps, prawns, mussels, cockles, oysters, big eyes, garoupa, young barracuda. Some of the fish are sold fresh; others are salted and dried. Once they have been sorted and prepared in lots for auction, the fishermen are able to collect their shares of the profits.

As Aberdeen's market is crowded with all kinds of fish, her harbor is crowded with innumerable large junks and small vessels, some of which never spread sail. Today, many of the houseboats can be seen with television sets on board. But if the scene does not compare to the Canton water scene of generations ago, it does have variety and color. There are floating shops, hawkers and small restaurants. Sampans display their wares of flowers, fruit and vegetables as they slowly cruise along the narrow lanes. The boats on which people live are veritable Noah's Arks, populated by chickens, dogs and rat-chasing cats. Children and pets are often assigned lucky names. A son may be named in hopes that he will bring great honor or fortune to his family; a daughter, whose arrival would be the cause of less celebration, might be called Dai-tai, which literally means "bring along a younger brother." Even the water changes color according to the weather's many moods: from pea green to a cold grey, from grey to a murky brown, from brown to a sparkling blue-green constantly reflecting the sun's rays.

While the men engage in fishing, the women and older children busily clean, cook, prepare the nets and watch over the very young. From an early age, a boy is expected to learn how to take over the ship in the event of emergency. Their heavy responsibility gives them a proud, self-reliant character and a love of freedom.

Not too many years ago, the fishermen employed a sorcerer known as Nam-mo-lo to frighten evil spirits from their vessels, as well as a specialist who, while deep in a trance, would learn why the gods were displeased. Today the fisherfolk seldom rely on the power of the gods to cure them of their illnesses. They are now quite willing to visit a doctor on Apleichau Island to obtain medical aid. The treatment and first aid courses are part of the program of the Hong Kong and Kowloon Floating Fisherman Welfare Promotion Association, established in 1964.

Although children dive expertly for coins tossed by tourists, about half the fisherfolk — especially the women — cannot swim. Most of the floating population are still married at sea, and land burial in Aberdeen's huge cemetery, overlooking the harbor, is far too expensive. The final voyage is made aboard a somber little coffin boat which conveys them to Cheung Chau Island for burial.

Color, form and contrast are provided by the rows of fish lined up to dry, the colorful decorations hung up at Chinese New Year and other festivals and by the many types of nets: long black nets draped over the masts of the seine-netting junks and snowy-white nets of the drift-netting junks. Small children may be seen aboard deck enjoying a ride on an improvised swing made from ropes; their naked younger brothers or sisters are kept from hazardous adventure by a harness anchored to a piece of furniture or a mast. It is an unfortunate fact that Aberdeen has more drownings involving children than anywhere else in Hong Kong.

The fisherfolk have always been extremely mobile. They would sell their catch in Macao or China or Hong Kong and return to the land only to anchor their boats, market their catch, mend their nets and bream their crafts. Few dared venture out over the land. With the progress of resettlement schemes, such self-reliance may be a thing of the past. Many of the floating population now welcome the move into resettlement estates; their fear of typhoons remains deep within them.

Although the size of the fishing fleet has decreased by almost half within the last 25 years, the remaining vessels are catching four times more fish. In 1951 there were 100 mechanized junks. Today, there are thousands. Officials responsible for streamlining the industry admit, with some regret, that the picturesque fishing junk with its beautiful sails is being deliberately sacrificed in the name of modern efficiency. As a consequence, the few junks with beautiful sails seen in Hong Kong waters are often from China, where progress has not yet made them obsolete.

The larger junks go out to sea (often into Chinese waters) for ten days or two weeks at a time; the smaller ones venture out into only one current. Their trip may last less than a day.

While on a fishing trip, the crew, usually consisting of a large family and the hired hands, may play mahjong, sleep, read, rest and listen to the radio. The schedule varies according to the method of fishing employed. The junks may leave in pairs about 2 in the morning and return at 8 in the evening of the same day. Several times a day the net is lowered into place for about four hours each time. The catch is later transferred to a special lighter which takes the fish to the Aberdeen Wholesale Fishmarket.

The fishermen now pack some of the fish in crushed ice and salt the large ones. A junk usually has a storeroom, fresh and salt fish holds, an ice hold, a fresh water tank, a galley, a W.C., an engine room, living compartments for family and hired crew members and a general hold. The shrine to Tin Hau is usually sited in the port cabin or in the kitchen near the engine room. The sleeping compartments are clean, tidy and invariably small. They usually consist of a small mat placed over a large flat wooden tray which serves as a bed, an electric light, a few pictures on the wall, boots and shoes and a few neatly folded articles of clothing. The compartments are barely high enough to permit squatting or sitting.

Evidence of modernization is seen everywhere aboard both the sea-going junks and those which remain within Hong Kong's coves and harbors. Fishermen who once made nets by twisting the string from fibrous grass on Aberdeen's hillsides now use nets of nylon; their children are learning to adopt the habits and attitudes of those on land, and tales of adventure of the awe-inspiring northeast monsoon in the South China Sea are not as popular as the latest film at the local theater. Wives who once mended nets now spend their efforts in keeping house on land.
Reliance on Lu Pan, the legendary master carpenter who introduced the secrets of shipbuilding, has shifted to trust in blueprints and templates. The poop deck's long free-swinging, hardwood tiller and huge perforated wooden rudder are disappearing in favor of a ship's wheel

Even in the early 1960s, junks in full sail were a common sight in Aberdeen Harbor. Calamities, such as fire and typhoon, have often plagued the people of Aberdeen. On October 30, 1971 a fire destroyed the still-uncompleted Jumbo Floating Restaurant and took 36 lives. Months before that disaster, 100-foot flames illuminated the night sky during a fire at Apleichau Island's power station. Fortunately, the boat population was unharmed.

and a much smaller steel rudder that turns on a metal shaft; the height of the poop has been lowered and powered winches are welded to the decks.

More attention is being given to Aberdeen than ever before. A long-term development scheme will eventually turn the region into a satellite town for Hong Kong. Reclaimed land will further diminish the size of the harbor, and large government housing complexes will accommodate many of the boat people. A proposed reclamation near the approaches to the bridge between the mainland and Apleichau will house a civic center. Thirty acres have been set aside for an oceanarium. Just to the west of Apleichau, Magazine Island may be developed as an amusement center.

Apleichau itself will undergo many changes. Its eastern coastline will have a Lamma Island Ferry Concourse. It will also have a new US$8 million resettlement estate housing 21,600 people. On the southern coastline, further reclamation is planned for the relocation of "offensive trades" from other areas of Hong Kong Island, including a refuse disposal incinerator. There are plans for a tunnel road from Aberdeen to Happy Valley which, by linking with the Cross Harbor Tunnel, will bring Aberdeen to one-half hour's driving distance from Kai Tak Airport.

In the past, government officials have remained flexible. During resettlement, the majority of fishing families has preferred to move from ship to shore; those more traditionally-minded who did not were allowed to moor elsewhere in the harbor. With more land reclamation from the sea, however, future resettlement schemes may not be able to allow the fishermen any alternative to land resettlement.

With the imminent modernization and industrialization of Aberdeen, it is obvious that a way of life is about to disappear. What will replace the last rays of its vanishing traditions is uncertain. But if, in the eclipse, the fishing junks with their beautiful butterfly-wing sails in russet, indigo and brown are made obsolete, it is because a more productive fleet is in the making; a fishing vessel uncluttered with children, pets and household belongings is a more efficient one. Future generations — whether on land or aboard ship — should have more secure, less adventurous livelihoods.

Historians tell us that piracy in Aberdeen waters dates to Mongol times, and the fury of the South China Sea was ever present. But, in the face of such familiar adversity, the independent character of the floating population only strengthened. Whether or not the uncompromising demands of progress will destroy what piratical raids and great winds could not, only the future can tell.

Progress has not been kind to Apleichau Island. The squatter huts that lined its hills in this 1963 photograph are gone, but the unsightly advertisements on buildings along the shore remain. Like all boat families, this mother and her children enjoy dinner on board their junk. This family soon may be eating its meals in a huge housing estate planned for Apleichau Island. A junk in full sail crossing Hong Kong Harbor is rapidly becoming one of the colony's rare attractions.

the portrait
from dawn to dusk

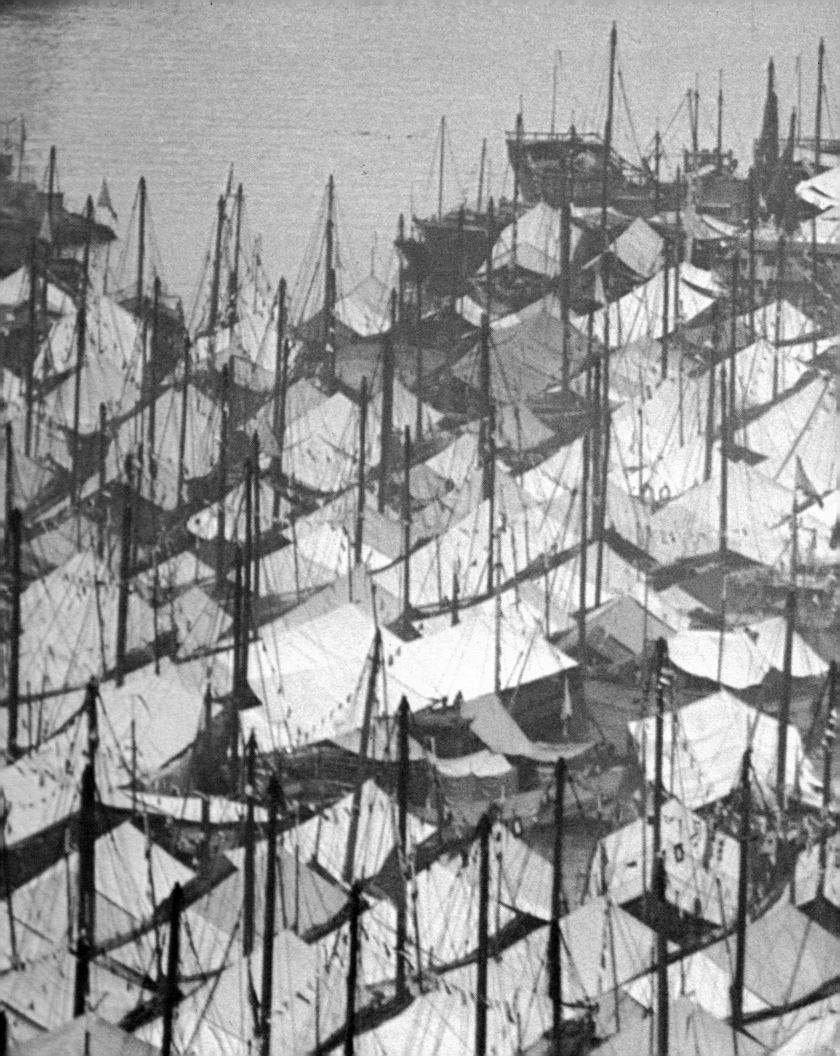

In the early morning hours, few of Aberdeen's fisherfolk are awake. The tall masts of their ships rise above hundreds of white canvas coverings like stately pines on a snow-mantled Chinese mountainside. The smoke of hundreds of breakfast fires blends with the early morning mist, creating the ethereal beauty of an Impressionist painting. At this time of day the modern diesel engines are silent. Aberdeen sleeps, as it did long ago when its only inhabitants were itinerant fishermen.

43

Warmed by the sun's rays, the harbor comes to life. A few early risers glide silently across the harbor in sampans, surrounded by seine-netters, long-liners, gill-netters, trawlers, floating restaurants and humble houseboats. From now until long after dark, the sampans never stop moving. Some become floating shops, filled with cooked food, fruits and vegetables or bolts of cloth. Others transport both people and goods between ship and shore. The harbor's mercurial light and capricious weather are reflected in the water's colors, swiftly creating and dispelling moods of disquietude or tranquillity.

51

The junks are the boat people's most valued possessions; throughout their history, their livelihood has depended on how skillfully they use them. The fish they catch, the clothing they wear and the nets they mend come next in importance. In addition to the weather and time of day, Aberdeen's kaleidoscope of color and form is provided by the constant movement of sampans and junks. As if painted by a master artist, the harbor scene is embellished by small but significant detail: multi-colored pennants flapping in the breeze, festival decorations lining the ships' sides, baskets of shrimp paste drying in the sun.

Aberdeen is more than meets the eye. There are the sounds of children tethered for safety to the mast and loudly crying for attention; dogs barking at fish flapping on the deck; boatbuilders shaping some of the world's finest junks; pea-green water lapping against a thousand bows. There is the feel of the toughest wood in the world: China fir, Brunei hardwood and teak. There is the smell of fish in baskets or jumping in nets or floating on the surface of the water. And there is the taste of dozens of varieties of seafood, cooked to perfection aboard the junks and in the gaily-colored floating restaurants.

Rows of junks, houseboats and sampans congest the harbor. Yet, already land reclaimed from the sea has taken its inevitable toll of Aberdeen. Fishermen say that there are now fewer boats and that the harbor is not as crowded as in years past; it is only that the reclaimed land has narrowed the harbor itself. Apleichau, or Goose Tongue Island (pages 74-75), is scheduled for further reclamation and modernization, including a resettlement estate for more than 20,000 people. The cemetery above the town of Aberdeen (page 77) is not used by the boat people. Land on Hong Kong Island is at a premium, and burial there is too expensive. Coffin boats take the fisherfolk on their last journey to a cemetery on Cheung Chau Island.

83

A magnificent sunset silhouettes the hulls of the junks against the harbor and gilds the rippled water. Although deeply conservative, the boat people are also practical. Like traditional Chinese everywhere, they attribute human strengths and weaknesses to their gods and goddesses. One folk tale speaks of a junk caught in a great rainstorm at sea. Despite the family's numerous prayers and offerings before the Queen of Heaven's shrine, the storm continued for days. In exasperation, the junk's captain removed the shrine and placed the goddess herself on deck to see how she liked such weather. The rain stopped.

84

After the collapse of the Manchu dynasty and throughout the turbulent years of the Republic of China, thousands of junks sailed down China's irregular coastline and made their way to the less troubled harbors of Hong Kong. There, they knew that if the government would do little to help them, at least it would not oppress them. After the occupation and devastation of the colony during World War II and the resultant bankruptcy of Aberdeen's population, the Hong Kong government began plans to aid the fishermen. Loans were granted and a fish marketing organization was set up to help the fishermen sell their catch at a fair price.

85

The congestion of the harbor leads to the constant passage across a junk's deck of families from neighboring vessels. Such proximity engenders both honesty and a willingness to help out with a neighbor's work. "Landlubbers" often speak disparagingly of the apparent contamination of the water. Aboard ship, however, the family head enforces rules of neatness and cleanliness far more rigid than those adhered to in the resettlement blocks on shore. The sampan is essential to the myriad waterborne activities in Aberdeen. It takes its name from *sam* (three) and *pan* (planks); many sampans are little more than that.

93

Within the shelter of Hong Kong waters, both work and play are carried on without fear of the weather. Clothes drying in the sun flutter above the furled sails; crew members dive, swim and relax aboard as would any boat owner on a sunny weekend. At sea, the fisherman may listen to weather reports broadcast from stations along the southern coast of China. His more modern and better educated children will read and listen to music. Both generations join in long and noisy games of mahjong. It is said that the boat people invented the ivory tiles used in the game as a substitute for cards, cards being too difficult to control on a windy sea.

In addition to the tourist attractions, there are other floating restaurants and halls in Aberdeen, such as the Floating Marriage Hall, where many boat people hold their weddings. These are seldom visited by foreigners, just as the large floating restaurants are seldom patronized by the fishermen. Someone reared in Aberdeen's floating village develops a strong sense of balance and rhythm from infancy — even while being carried by his mother on the planks of sampans and on the decks of junks.

By 5 a.m., Aberdeen's wholesale fishmarket is bustling. Dozens of workers sort the fish into baskets in preparation for the day's auctions. In the interest of efficiency, auctions are yielding to negotiated sales. Big eyes, young barracuda, shark, shrimps, prawns, crabs, mussels, sea weeds, red sea bream, golden thread, sea snakes, manta rays... After the auction, the fishermen collect their shares.

To the land people, the fisherman's way of life was strange. Like gipsies everywhere, the sea gipsies were scorned and ridiculed. It was said that their feet had six toes, their eyes could see the ferocious creatures lurking in the sea's murky depths and that they could swim beneath the surface for miles without air and without rest.

Although fish prices are rising, the higher cost of fuel, labor and material makes for steadily dwindling profits. Even without resettlement, the fisherman's way of life is thus endangered. The price of junks has increased by nearly 50 per cent in recent years. In the face of spiraling costs, the fisherman's catch simply cannot provide for his family and pay off a loan on a new junk. Aberdeen's boatyards turn out more than a dozen different kinds, in lengths of 35 to 95 feet.

In many of Aberdeen's boatyards, traditional and modern methods exist side by side. Elderly master carpenters, who can neither read nor write, follow the building techniques they learned in China over half a century ago and which have changed little since Marco Polo described them during his sojourn in China. While admitting great respect for the skill of the masters, younger apprentices now follow plans and templates. Each boatyard has its small corner shrine to Lu Pan, the patron saint of the boatbuilders. Stories, hundreds of years old, tell of the saint appearing in the disguise of a poor laborer to aid shipbuilders in solving problems of construction. Lu Pan's methods of shipbuilding are now rapidly being discarded in favor of blueprints and modern industrial techniques.

115

Like all Chinese, the boat people find it difficult to conceal parental pride in their children. Yet early in life the young are left alone to entertain themselves and to take care of still younger brothers and sisters. Qualities of self-reliance and leadership are quickly developed. Old customs die hard. The child in the picture above is a boy disguised as a girl. His mother knows that the evil spirits are not interested in females; hence, she protects her sons with feminine hair styles and feminine nicknames.

120

On junks and houseboats, space is limited and every article on board must be useful. The tires hanging on the sides of the boats are used to cushion landings against a pier, as well as to take the shock out of collisions. There is little need to be jealous of a neighbor's wealth. A boat with a television set is soon crowded by dozens of neighbors who cannot yet afford their own. Children whose parents were brought up on stories of the beautiful moon maiden now watch American spaceships land on the moon. Without this "good neighbor" policy, Aberdeen could probably not survive. Rather than envy another family's new junk, neighbors join in celebrations and banquets over this good fortune.

122

Even Aberdeen's children speak of the joy felt when, after a long and anxious wait, they see the net emerge slowly from the water, swollen with hundreds of fat, thrashing fish. As practice makes perfect, the harbor itself is a good place to learn. Years of training give the young men confidence and expertise for fishing expeditions; and years of carrying children on their backs give the girls a superb posture. Some of Aberdeen's children have learned that begging or selling souvenirs to tourists may bring in spending money. Until recently, the practice was carried out clandestinely, well away from family elders. However, with financial disaster imminent, the boat families may have little choice. It is, after all, their way of life which is the real tourist attraction. Why, they may ask, should only others benefit?

125

Furrowed lines are etched deeply into this fisherman's handsome, copper-brown face. Years of serving none but himself have left him confident and independent. Years of being an outcast from those on land have left him suspicious and stoical. Years of struggle have made him sympathetic and generous to anyone in need. His face reflects his sense of humor, of melancholy, and, above all, of pride. He is relaxed in memories of his heroic encounters with the sea, and anxious over rumored resettlement schemes looming above his sails like a darkening sky.

Whether at work or at play, the children of Aberdeen are always active. In the picture above, the boat children work on their father's junk. In the background spreads the enormous Wah Fu Estate, symbolic of the probable destiny of the children. Occasionally, some of the fishermen's sails are tattered and torn to the point that there seems precious little fabric left to catch the wind. Such sails are often patched with whatever material is available, creating a sail of contrasting colors and unusual designs. Aberdeen's boat children soon become expert at diving for coins and navigating small boats. The construction of a Chinese opera platform snares the interest of the boat people.

136

Although films and television programs compete with the demand for Chinese opera, the operatic companies find a ready welcome among the fisherfolk. During festivals of the boat people, the operas are frequently held aboard a junk. The dragon chasing the ball is a common Chinese motif, and is sometimes interpreted as China chasing the Pearl of Wisdom. Great battles and heroic deeds are the most popular themes of Chinese operas.

138

The most important patron saint of the fisherfolk is *Tin Hau,* the Queen of Heaven. Her temples are built along the shore so that she can watch out over the water. Festivals in her honor should also be carried out within her view, lest she grow angry at being excluded. Reclamation in Aberdeen has placed both land and buildings between the Tin Hau Temple and the harbor. Many elderly fishermen say that today's developments, such as resettlement schemes and polluted waters, are the result of careless treatment of their Queen of Heaven, who can no longer look out upon the water to protect her people.

Fortunately, the boat people have as many gods protecting them as they have dangers confronting them. If a ship is lost, offerings can be made to the goddess known as "Thousand Mile Eyes" to aid in the search. If assurance of good weather is needed before a long fishing voyage, supplicants need only insure that earnest prayers are said before the goddess known as "Fair Wind Ears." Rituals may also be carried out on the junk itself, usually before paintings of Chinese gods, the Eight Immortals remaining the most popular.

It is during festivals that the floating population embroiders a tapestry of old-world beauty. Celebrations include performances of Chinese opera, lion dances, smoldering joss sticks, offerings of sacrificial roast pigs covered with banners and flowers, chickens, dishes of pink buns and baskets of red eggs and money. Near the temple, but far from the eyes of officials, enterprising young men set up their games of chance. Everywhere there are color, music and, above all, feasts and banquets. Even fireworks, now forbidden throughout Hong Kong, mysteriously appear at every festival, invoking the blessings of the fishermen's gods and goddesses. A priest is not necessary when an offering is made, as is the case with land-dwellers. The head of a fishing family may conduct the rituals himself.

144

Each junk has its own honored shrine dedicated to the Queen of Heaven. She is often placed in the port cabin before a candle or small light. On the 23rd day of the 3rd moon, pilgrims make their way to dozens of temples along the shores of Hong Kong and those of the outer islands. Many of the old customs are disappearing, such as introducing all new children to the goddess and promising vast quantities of eggs for the birth of a male child. But each festival still sees hundreds of junks sailing out of Hong Kong's harbors to pay respect to their patron saint.

145

The *fa pau* wood and paper decorations are both elaborate and expensive. They are carried ashore and placed before the Goddess of Heaven. As more junks arrive, the room becomes crowded with these beautiful offerings, made especially for the celebration. The shrines to Tin Hau are taken from their places of honor aboard the junks and brought on shore. The junks are all gaily decorated with brightly colored pennants, streamers and floral screens. Lion Dance performers keep up a constant din of cymbals and drums even before they reach the shore. In some parts of Hong Kong, entranced mediums still communicate with the gods and interpret their wishes.

Like their counterparts on land, the waterfolk
celebrate important Chinese festivals. The Dragon
Boat Festival is held in commemoration of the
suicide of Chu Yuan, a poet and statesman who
lived more than 2,000 years ago. Chu Yuan fell
victim to an intrigue, which also resulted in the
collapse of his kingdom. Despairing of influencing
his Emperor, on the fifth day of the fifth moon he
drowned himself in the Mek Lo River. The villagers
set out in boats searching for his body. In hopes
that the fish would not molest Chu Yuan's corpse,
they scattered rice in the water and chanted
prayers.

156

As Chu Yuan's death was unjust, it became
necessary to appease his restless spirit. Every year,
on the fifth day of the fifth moon, boats patrolled
the river and rice was thrown into the water.
Chu Yuan's fame spread along with the custom.
Today, the tragedy of his death has evolved
into the colorful dragon boat regatta and the
consumption of specially-made glutinous
puddings. The once-unadorned patrol boats are
now bedecked with flags and banners; fierce,
finely-carved dragons serve as their figureheads.

157

Every locality does its best to enter a boat in the Dragon Boat race. Dozens of rowers crowd into the long, slender craft, sitting in pairs. As the drums are rhythmically beaten, the rowers strive to paddle energetically and in coordination. Although elderly residents of Aberdeen insist that today's celebrations are far less elaborate than those of long ago, the Dragon Boat races are still days of great crowds and festive merriment.

In addition to the thousands of junks, houseboats and other vessels that moor in Aberdeen, thousands more pass through, using the harbor as shelter or as a place to sell their catch or mend their nets. It is this constant coming and going of vessels which makes an accurate count almost impossible. In the rays of the setting sun, even the grotesqueness of Apleichau Island's power station fails to spoil Aberdeen's mood of enchantment.

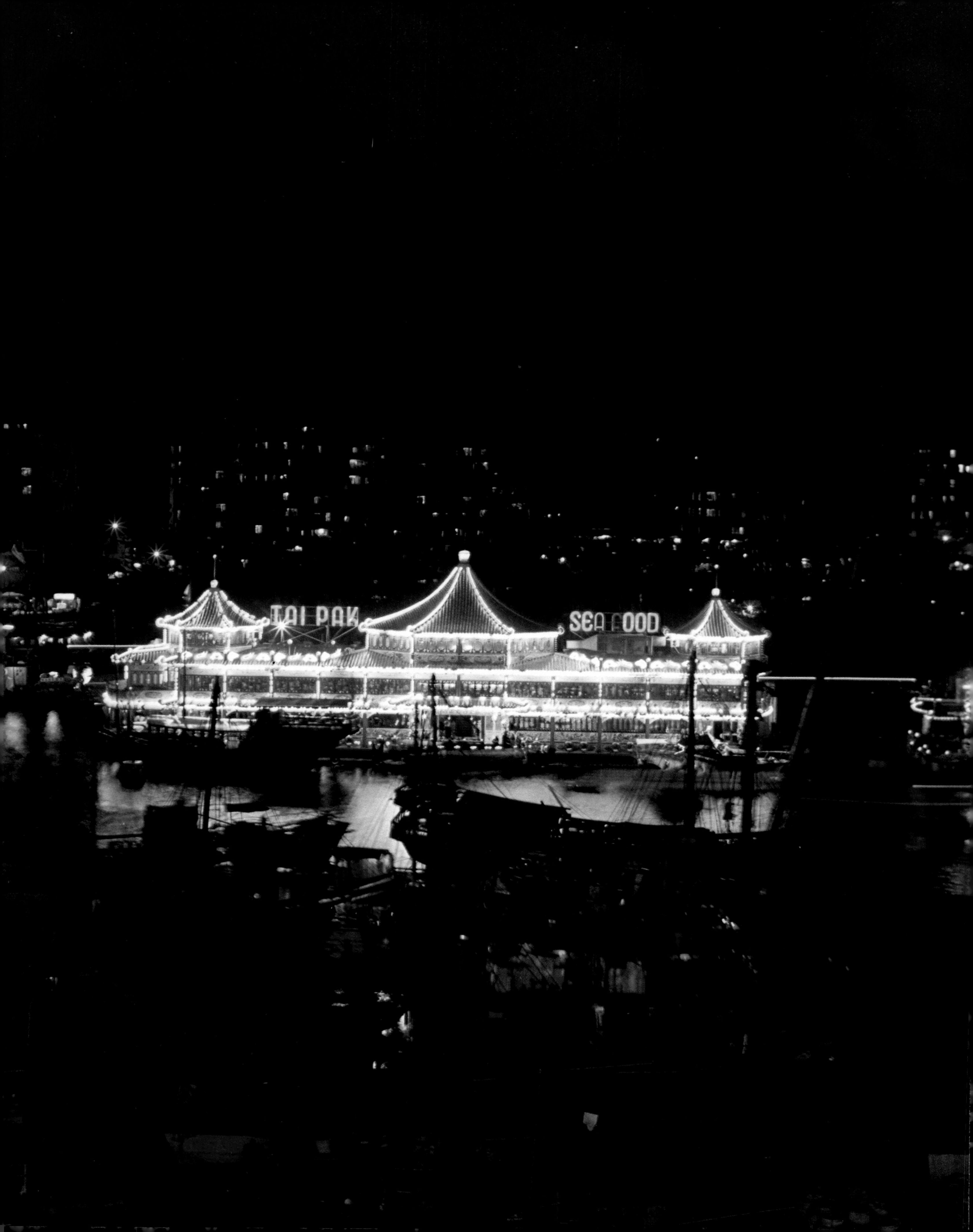
TAI PAK
SEA FOOD

Aberdeen's two floating restaurants, the Tai Pak and the Sea Palace, are still the main tourist attractions in Aberdeen. Their ornate decor follows the style of traditional Chinese palaces. The two restaurants will soon be joined by an even larger Jumbo Floating Restaurant. As Aberdeen's sky turns from red to violet to dark purple, huge neon signs and rows of multi-colored lightbulbs emblazon the water with color, adding a bewitching magic to Aberdeen's nocturnal beauty.

185

the people
7 interviews

At 72, Ch'en Chu-hua has the eyes of a man who has spent a lifetime at sea. His face is furrowed and tanned, and the eyes, so accustomed to looking across the wide expanses of the South China Sea, have borrowed the color of the ocean.

Chu-hua doesn't remember if he was born on land or on a junk, but he does remember taking his bride aboard a junk more than 40 years ago. At that time there was no such thing as the Aberdeen floating marriage hall. During the ceremony, an orange plant, symbol of good fortune and many sons, was placed in the center of the junk. After the ceremony ended, the plant was moved to the stern and his married life began.

He remembers when, years ago, fishermen gladly bought unwanted boy children and then immediately began teaching them the fishing trade. But he is quite certain that the practice of child-buying has now died out.

Chu-hua only chuckles when the subject of modern fishing equipment is mentioned. He knows that awards have been given to inventors of machines which, it is said, aid the fishermen. He mouths a raucous oath and spits contemptuously. "What need have I for a depth-finder when for generations my family has told depths with the use of a string? How could a better radar be invented than the sun? Do I need a machine to tell me when the weather will change?"

The outline of Chu-hua's junk could not be more traditional. Yet, despite its appearance, he admits that he has allowed his sons to modernize it "a bit." When its diesel engines and twin-screw propellers are in use, the sail is seldom hoisted. Its fish-hold has been fitted with modern insulation material; a ship's wheel and steel rudder have replaced the wooden tiller and wooden rudder. He frankly admits he misses the huge free-swinging tiller and regrets having made the change.

Chu-hua's junk usually pairs with another. Together they leave about 2 a.m. and return at 8 p.m. the same day. Sometimes, trips may last a week or more. While fishing, Chu-hua sleeps, rests and listens to the radio. Three times a day the net is put down for about four hours each time. The catch — mainly golden thread and lizard fish — is then transferred to a smaller vessel which takes the fish to the market.

His sons have heard rumors that they are to be resettled, but neither he nor his two sons want to leave the junk and live on shore. Chu-hua cannot understand how people on the land ever find happiness and the feeling of freedom. He asks: "Who wants to live like fish in a hold?"

Chu-hua sees all resettlement schemes as a curse of the fisherfolk. He points toward the shore as if it were a South China Sea monsoon. "Of course we're cursed. Aberdeen's Tin Hau Temple was originally built on the shore, but land reclamation has pushed it inland. Now the goddess inside can no longer watch out over us. Resettlement is our just punishment!"

He admits that some of the changes are for the best: "With the sail and a strong wind, no one aboard a junk had much sleep. Now, with the engine, it is different. And, in years past, fishermen were seldom out of debt."

His son reminds him it's time for his rest. As he rises, Chu-hua looks with obvious pride at his son and then turns to us. "Fishing is a hard life. These days, if a man has five sons, only one or two will choose to make fishing his way of life. But the ones who do will know what it means to be boss of their own boat."

191

"Yes, I think it's easier. I think life on shore is less strenuous. I don't fear the storms any more like I did on my husband's trawler. And my children can go to school. And, of course, now I don't have to worry about them falling into the water. But, still, it doesn't seem we're together as much as we were then. We used to eat together, fish together, and — well, I guess we did just about everything together. But not now. Now the children are in school, my husband is working in the factory and I clean our two rooms by myself."

Mrs. Leung's face is still the copper brown of all boat people. And even after two years in a resettlement estate, away from the open sea, it readily breaks into a friendly and relaxed smile.

At first, she found it difficult to adapt to life on land. Her children would occasionally overhear other children, born on land, deriding them as sea-born rustics. Since life at sea did not prepare the Leungs for jobs on land and how to behave there, they found it hard to cope with the demands made upon them. The children cried often and wanted to return to the sea.

But that was impossible. With only four children, she and her husband would have had to hire others to man their boat. Those with few children, such as Mrs. Leung, now leave the sea to work in the factories. Her husband could not afford the rapidly rising costs of repairing his ship, the higher wages for help and the higher cost of fuel. "Of course, the price of fish has also gone up rapidly, but most of the profit goes right to the wholesaler, not the fishermen. And, although the profits decline, the work remains as demanding as always."

Mrs. Leung's husband now works in a shoe factory in Aberdeen from 8 a.m. to 8 p.m., six days a week. The hours are more regular than those of a fisherman, the work is less tiring. And the income is known in advance so Mrs. Leung can now plan their expenditures carefully.

She is quick to point out the disadvantages of her new life-style. She is upset by the lawlessness on land and the lack of kindness between neighbors. "Each person is in his own special place and isn't so ready to help the next." And her own two small rooms allotted to her and her family are not pleasant. The smell from the communal toilet permeates the rooms, the din of a dozen families enters from the dark hallway.

Many of her older friends wish to stay aboard ship, but she knows that many of their children do not oppose the move to shore. She and her husband did not take the decision lightly. Only after her husband's catch could no longer support them did they consider resettlement. Mrs. Leung and her husband blame the pollution in Hong Kong waters for forcing the fish to move elsewhere. And she says that the bad weather over the last few years has contributed to a reduction in the catch of all the fishermen, a fact borne out by the statistics of the Agriculture and Fisheries Department. She feels that intensive fishing on the Continental Shelf has caused the number of fish to decline there also. Although this belief is widespread among fishermen, the Department finds nothing to sustain their claims of over-fishing on the Shelf.

Mrs. Leung is still well-informed about fishing activities. She has heard that the Agriculture and Fisheries Department's 239-ton fisheries research vessel Cape St. Mary has located a new fishing ground approximately 400 miles south of Hong Kong. But like most fishermen, her husband's friends are reluctant to leave the area they have known all their lives.

The case of Mrs. Leung and her husband is reflected in the official statistics. In 1971 there were 50,000 working fishermen in Hong Kong. In 1972, there were 45,000. The number is expected to drop with each successive year.

Mrs. Leung leaves her resettlement block with us. She needs to shop before her husband returns. "Now, I buy food from the market," she says. "Before, we would often have our meal served up from a floating sampan cooked-food stall." Briefly she glances toward the harbor. She tells us that on Sundays with her husband, and sometimes during the week when she feels lonely, she walks down to the harbor and onto the vessels of her former neighbors to talk of the past. She admits to feeling a bit strange now in this once-familiar place. And she remembers the sway of the ship and the salt spray and the excitement of seeing nets full of fish emerge from the dark water. Her smile is wistful. "That excitement is something that must be experienced to be understood."

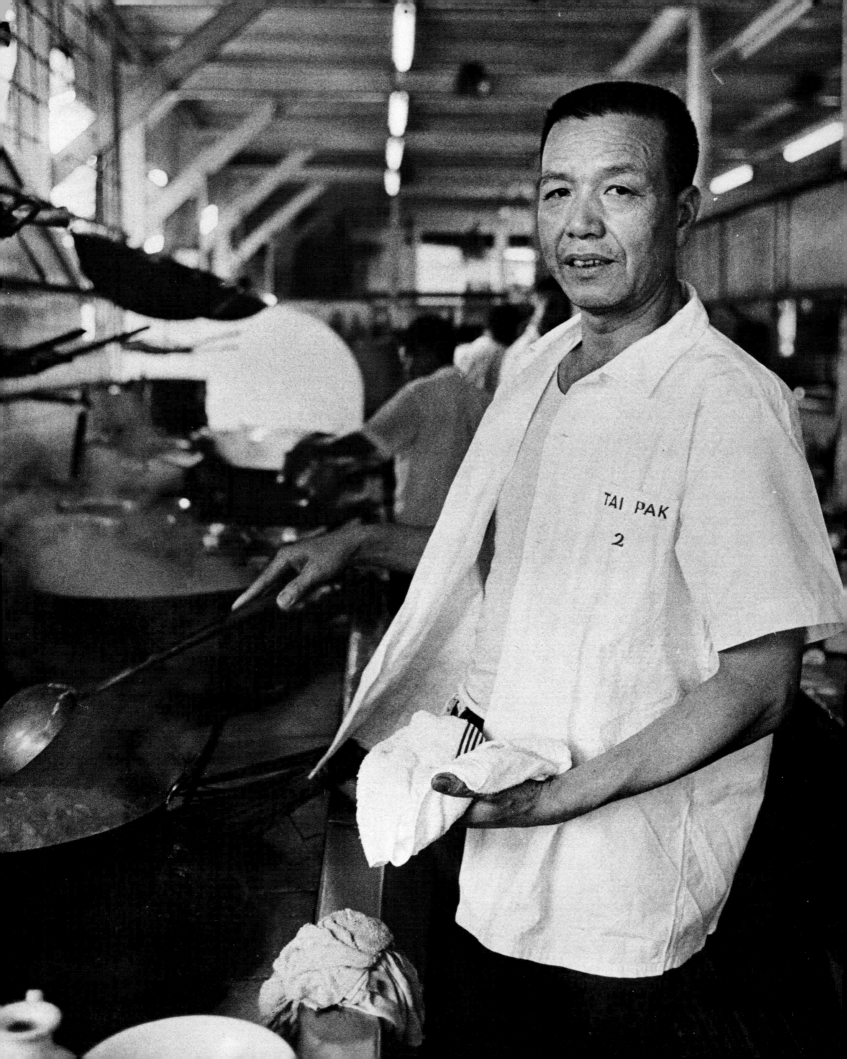

Yip-lam, 49, knows fish. He knows their color, texture, scent, value and, above all else, the exact time each fish needs in preparation before its taste is perfect. For nearly a quarter century he has been a cook in Aberdeen's Tai Pak Floating Restaurant. As a child he followed his uncle about the kitchens of restaurants in Kwangtung province. It was from his uncle that he first acquired the pride all professional chefs display in their work.

Six and a half days a week, from 11 a.m. to 11 p.m., Yip-lam and 31 others work in the kitchen. After a lifetime of long hours he is quite used to it. But when he returns to his small Aberdeen apartment, he has little time for hobbies or other diversions. His wife and four children offer prayers and incense at temples during festivals and, of course, play mahjong with their neighbors. For Yip-lam, seeing a film two or three times a year is the extent of his entertainment.

He is a man completely happy in his work, which he finds both creative and relaxing. He can talk about it for hours: "Aberdeen's most popular fish are the garoupa and the snapper. Steamed prawns must be live and are therefore the fastest of all to prepare; like all seafood, they must never be overcooked. Lobster dishes are the most time-consuming. Not many fish can be kept beyond a few days."

Most of Yip-lam's dishes are not prepared for the gourmet; rather they are chosen by representatives of travel services who order them for their tourist groups. He regrets that the decision is not his. Sometimes, however, a connoisseurs' banquet is held at which only the finest dishes are acceptable. The kitchen staff comes to life and begins the energetic preparation of exotic dishes, including genuine shark's fin soup, which may cost up to HK$1,000 for a table of six.

Yip-lam smiles wryly and uses his finger to make a point. "A few people complain that our prices are not all on the menus. But, with fish prices going up so fast, we'd have to print up new menus every day. The price of shrimp increased 50 per cent in six months and crabs went up almost as much! And each season brings a new price. Our restaurant has its own fishermen from whom we buy most of our fish, but if there is a shortage, we occasionally buy from others."

Over the years, Yip-lam has seen many of his friends' sons go abroad to work as cooks. After they gain experience, they return to work in Aberdeen's restaurants. His own son once worked in a restaurant on land. For the last three years he has worked with his father in the Tai Pak's kitchen. Like his father, he has learned the different procedures for each category of customers. He knows better than to turn a fish over at a fishermen's banquet; the gesture is too similar to a boat capsizing. And fishermen do not mind waiting patiently for a worthwhile meal. On the other hand, he knows that many tourists come mainly to see Aberdeen's floating population and have neither the time for nor the interest in an ambrosial feast.

Yip-lam explains the easy-going attitudes of himself and the other cooks with a knowing smile. "There is something about the open kitchen and the water and the sun that is quite different from a kitchen in a restaurant on land. It is difficult to be depressed or sullen — even when a fish doesn't cook well."

In many ways, Kuo Chin-sheng's appearance is typical of the young men of the floating population. His face reflects his strong character, his body lacks any trace of softness and the soles of his feet are leathery from leaping across wooden decks.

A small green jade goddess of mercy hangs around his neck. His blue jeans and T-shirt are faded but clean. He is pleased that the value of jade and the price of shrimp keep increasing.

He was born in Hong Kong 20 years ago. While still a boy, he began working with his father, now retired aboard a junk. He is the oldest of five brothers and two sisters. Chin-sheng works aboard a shrimp-catching junk and earns about HK$800 a month, plus room and board.

He spends 10 or 15 days at sea, then rests for two days between trips. The shrimp they catch is put into the hold where there is room for more than 30 large wooden barrels. As soon as they return to Hong Kong waters, the barrels are transferred to a barge which takes the shrimp into Hong Kong island's Central District.

As is the case with many of Aberdeen's junks, the sail is seldom used. All junks are required to carry a sail in the event of engine failure. But Chin-sheng knows that the sail is torn and soiled from remaining unfurled for weeks on end and is probably useless.

With the widespread installation of diesel engines, there is now less fear of typhoons; Chin-sheng is able to go to sea 12 months of the year. He eats three meals a day of fish, beans, pork, rice and vegetables. But fresh vegetables do not keep for long; on a long trip he usually goes without this item of his diet.

Chin-sheng is treated almost as a member of his master's family. He sleeps on a mat in one of the four small cubicles at the stern. Each "bedroom" usually sleeps two or three people.

His own room consists of two sleeping mats, a bare light bulb, neatly piled clothing and boots and a few personal belongings. It is impossible to stand; even sitting is accomplished with difficulty.

The sleeping room of the ship's master is similar but includes linoleum on the floor and pictures of a youthful Chairman Mao on the walls. Chin-sheng explains that the junks fish in Chinese waters and often enter Chinese ports. They sometimes give part of their catch to China. Like many of the junk owners, his captain holds dual licenses, one from China and one from Hong Kong.

Besides the hold, the junk also has a storeroom, motor-room and small galley area with a shrine to Tin Hau.

Even at 20, Chin-sheng can accurately predict the weather. He also listens to weather reports from radio stations along the China coast. Besides the radio, his entertainment consists of mahjong and reading. The children aboard the junk have no toys and are left to amuse themselves aboard the ship. They also play with the dog and the cat. The latter is often found aboard a junk in almost constant pursuit of the rats. The small children are sometimes tethered to the mast or to a chair or else fitted with an improvised life belt made of wood.

A small, almost naked boy appears in a cubicle doorway. Except for a long tuft of hair, his head has been shaved. His facial appearance and dress are those of a girl. Chin-sheng explains that the owner's wife is superstitious. She believes in ghosts and in evil spirits who might attempt to possess her sons. Hence, the two youngest boys are not only dressed as girls but are also given temporary feminine names. It seems that spirits, evil or otherwise, are not interested in girls. When the junk is moored in Aberdeen during a typhoon, the children are sent to stay with friends on the land.

Chin-sheng recognizes the troubles ahead for those who fish the South China Sea. The rising cost of diesel fuel makes fishing less profitable. And he worries about what effects the proposed Lamma Island oil refinery will have on Hong Kong waters. Despite such fears, he has no interest in being resettled. In a few years he hopes to get a loan from the government or from friends of his father to enable him to buy his own boat. He explains that if the merchant fishermen feel that the borrower is honest, muscular and healthy enough and can probably catch enough fish to repay the loan, large sums can be borrowed. Chin-sheng should have no trouble.

Wong-kao, who is 45, rises at 4:30 every morning of the week. He leaves his small apartment and walks through the quiet, still-dark streets to the Aberdeen Wholesale Fish Market. He enters the canteen, orders tea and rice, and begins talking with the other fish buyers and fish sellers who, in a short while, will begin participating in the first of four loud and sometimes boisterous auctions. While Wong-kao and his friends eat their breakfast, they discuss the subject which, for most of them, has been their livelihood.

"Did you hear the news? Another fish farm was robbed last night. You'll see. Fish will soon be worth their weight in gold!"

"No wonder. The Japanese are offering our wholesalers more money to try to buy Hong Kong fish. I think their fish are already too polluted to eat. That's why prices are so high."

"It's not really the Japanese. It's the festival preparations. The fishermen can't catch fish and make decorations and offerings at the same time. Fish prices go up this time every year."

"Nonsense. Two years ago golden thread went for $3.35 (HK) a catty, remember? A year later it was only about ten cents more. But this year it's already reached $5. Mackerel, garoupa, all of them — prices have jumped sky high! They won't go down."

After breakfast the buying begins. Wong-kao's experienced eyes scan the long rows of yellow baskets. His fish and meat shop in Wongtaisin needs large supplies of garoupa and white pomfret. But there are other popular varieties. He watches as they are brought in, sorted and weighed: golden thread, yellow belly, melon coat, red goatfish, fork-tail, melon seed, red snapper, ginkgo, scads, lizard fishes, crevalles, conger-pike eels, big-eyes, mackerels, sardines, hair-tails, horse-heads, soles, croakers, anchovies, breams, snappers, round herrings, sharks, squid, cuttlefish and prawns, large and small.

Wong-kao checks carefully to see if the deep sea trawler's fish are fresh. He doesn't worry about those brought in by the long-liners and gill-netters. He knows their fish are the freshest of all. The fish will be sold at auction or, in the interests of efficiency, by negotiated sales. Slips of paper with the buyers' names begin to appear in several baskets of fish. And, in a few others, buyers have illegally sprinkled specially-colored confetti, signifying their intention to buy those particular baskets. By noon or one o'clock, the auctions are over. Wong-kao returns to his shop.

Although he was born in Hong Kong, he learned his trade from his father, a fish buyer in Kwangtung province. He puts in another full day from early afternoon until evening; supporting a wife, three sons and two daughters is not easy. His few holidays each year are on festival days and, as he is a Buddhist, he accompanies his wife and children to a temple.

Wong-kao knows the market takes a six per cent commission to cover handling charges. He doesn't complain. Since it is a non-profit organization, profits are used in granting loans to fishermen or else as aid to their children's schools. The first wholesale fish market was opened in 1945. From the Aberdeen Wholesale Market, the fish are distributed to retail markets. The great majority of locally landed fish are now directly loaded at the seven markets in Aberdeen, Shau Kei Wan, Cheung Sha Wan, Sai Kung, Tai Po, Sha Tau Kok and Castle Peak. Cheung Chau Island, Lantao Island and Stanley on Hong Kong Island all have fish collecting depots.

Certain innovations have been introduced to expedite the off-loading and sorting of fish. The fishermen themselves are now encouraged to pre-sort catches at sea, and to use especially designed plastic containers for use on board fishing vessels. The results are fresher fish and faster distribution.

Wong-kao's friends point out that Wong-kao has ample reason to be perpetually smiling. The prices of fish continue to rise almost daily, and one of his sons is now beginning to learn his trade. Wong-kao is a happy man.

When, as a young girl, Lai Kum-choi first began sculling passengers around Aberdeen Harbor on her sampan, the waters bore only fishing junks and other vessels; there were no floating restaurants or water tours catering to tourists. Today, Kum-choi (her name means "gold and wealth") still rows fishermen and their families between ship and shore; occasionally she also transports cargo. But increasingly her small, sheltered boat is hired by tourists for an hour's sightseeing around Aberdeen. She represents the third generation of sampan rowers in her family: both her mother and her grandmother worked the sampans.

Like most sampan workers, she owns her own boat. Years ago, when she bought it, sampans cost about HK$1,000. Now, with rising labor costs, the price is HK$3,000.

Kum-choi was born in Aberdeen and remembers how, as a little girl aboard a junk at sea, the huge waves would make her seasick. As she grew up, she continued working aboard the boats of Aberdeen and, as expected, married a young man who worked on a junk. Her marriage took place in Aberdeen's floating marriage hall, which today is still moored less than 50 yards from where she waits for customers. At the memory of her wedding, her attractive face breaks into a smile. "It was about the same as weddings on land," she says. "But there were three days of feasts instead of just one."

She remembers when a young man in search of a wife would do a bit of advertising by placing a pot of grass on the poop deck of the family junk. When a pot of flowers was similarly displayed on another junk, a marriage was in the making. At that time girls wore long, neatly-plaited pigtails to indicate that they were single. Today, it is simply one of many hair styles and has lost this significance.

At Kum-choi's wedding, guests were careful not to salute one another with cheers of "bottoms up." The fisherfolk believe the gesture to be one of ill omen, suggesting as it does that a boat might one day capsize.

Kum-choi works seven days a week. During the summer, when many people from the land seek the relative coolness of Aberdeen's waters, she is kept busy from 8 in the morning to midnight. But during the cooler winter months, business is slack and she may stop work at sunset.

Until three years ago, she and her family lived on one of the many small junks which never leave the harbor. But the government was intent on reclaiming the area where several junks were moored, including her own; so they were moved into a resettlement estate. Kum-choi is pleased that, except for the cost of textbooks, her children receive free schooling. But she and her family still prefer living aboard the junk, where there was more room and no rent to pay.

Although none of the sampans leave the immediate area of Aberdeen's harbor, she assures her passengers that flat-bottomed sampans with arched roofs such as her own are well balanced; her wicker settees are comfortable.

She and her husband are Buddhists. But except for festivals and holidays they seldom participate in religious observances. And, like many of the fisherfolk, Kum-choi is not without superstitions. She watched the huge, uncompleted Jumbo Floating Restaurant go up in flames on October 30, 1971. Thirty-six people lost their lives. Kum-choi is certain that their ghosts survive. Since the deaths were accidental, the ghosts are regarded as "unwilling" spirits and their presence can be strongly felt despite offerings made to propitiate them. She also believes that the roast pigs offered to fishermen's gods at festivals are decidedly lighter on their return trip, as the gods have absorbed the "essence" of the pigs.

When she was younger the channel was much wider, nor was there so much congestion in the harbor as there is today. Business was much better. People paid less for sampan rides, but the cost of living was lower then. It was much easier for the sampan workers to make a living. As we leave, Kum-choi brushes a bit of dirt from her otherwise spotless white *sam-fu*. "You can be sure," she says with a smile, "that my children will not work a sampan."

His alert eyes look out from a sunburned face; his hands move freely to emphasize his words. See-tu Fu, now 67, has been building boats since he was 16. He was born in China and first began working in boatyards there. He has worked in Apleichau Island's Safe and Reliable Shipyard for the last ten years. To the other workers he is known as "the old master." It is his skill which ensures the high quality of each boat produced.

His surname is one of only a few Chinese family names with two Chinese characters instead of one. As he talks, he climbs spryly about narrow planks and makeshift ladders overseeing the building of an 80-foot junk.

He hesitates before answering the question of how long it takes to build a junk. "There are many types of junks and job time depends on the weather. It is dangerous to work around electrical equipment when it is raining. But, in general, we can do the hull and topside construction of an 80-foot fishing junk in two months. It may last for 30 years.

"Almost all ships built at Aberdeen shipyards are fishing junks. A few pleasure craft are built for foreigners who are always in a hurry. Nobody orders boats to live on any more. Those living on boats are being resettled on the land."

Fu remembers how in his youth he would help paint eyes on the bows of the Fukienese boats. The owners believed that the eye could help find the fish. Today, he is never asked to add an eye to a bow.

One thing has remained unchanged, however: Fu's method of building. He still employs the same eye and rule-of-thumb methods he was taught in China half a century ago.

Even his method of modifying the hulls to accommodate modern machinery involves no plans, templates or blueprints.

Fu has heard that classes in modern boat design are held in Aberdeen. He shrugs. "Maybe for young men it's all right. But my methods have been used for generations. I cannot change now. Besides, I would have to learn to read and write."

The timber used in junk building is naturally the toughest available: teak, China fir and Brunei hardwoods. The planks are hewn in mills near the boatyards and curved by weighing down the ends with stones and applying the heat of a small fire to their centers. Fu tells us that during the last year, rising labor and material costs have increased the cost of a junk by 20 per cent.

Customers usually give Fu the materials and measurements of length and width. But the buyers know Fu's junks are well balanced and safe, so the exact design is left largely to him.

A small shrine in the corner of the shipyard is dedicated to Lu Pan, the legendary master carpenter who introduced the secrets of shipbuilding to the world. The 13th day of the sixth moon is Lu Pan's birthday, and it is one of the few days in the year on which Fu takes a rest.

He admits he doesn't particularly like having too many days to himself. His thoughts then begin to stray to his wife in China, whom he has not seen for many years.

Fu understands that the days of shipbuilding without plans and blueprints are numbered. He has seen the younger men forego old-fashioned tools, such as hand drills, in favor of modern power saws and electric drills. He knows modern anti-fouling paint protects the wood much longer than his method of using bundles of burning hay, a process known as breaming. But he is unconvinced that the younger workers have a genuine love for the work.

It seems obvious that when Fu's generation is gone, the shipbuilding methods described by Marco Polo 700 years ago will also die with it.